Original title:
Smiles in the Shadows of Dreams

Copyright © 2025 Swan Charm
All rights reserved.

Author: Paulina Pähkel
ISBN HARDBACK: 978-9908-1-4858-8
ISBN PAPERBACK: 978-9908-1-4859-5
ISBN EBOOK: 978-9908-1-4860-1

Serene Brightness in the Veil of Sleep

In the quiet of night, whispers flow,
Gentle dreams dance, soft and slow.
Stars weave stories, silver and bright,
Guiding us softly through the night.

Moonlight spills over, a silken grace,
Cradling whispers in a warm embrace.
Restful hearts find solace near,
In the serene glow, all is clear.

Slumber wraps us in tender light,
While shadows fade, taking flight.
Cocooned in peace, we drift away,
To realms where hope and love will sway.

With dawn's first breath, dreams will fade,
Yet in our hearts, they still cascade.
Serene brightness guides our way,
Through each new dawn, each vibrant day.

Joyful Secrets Beneath the Dreamscape

In gardens lush, where wishes bloom,
Secrets nestle, dispelling gloom.
In playful colors, laughter sings,
Joy unravels on airy wings.

Beneath the stars, we spin and sway,
With every twinkle, night turns to day.
Dreams lay hidden, waiting to tell,
Of magical lands, where spirits dwell.

Wildflowers giggle in softest hues,
While gentle breezes hum their muse.
Each sigh a secret, each glance a song,
In this dreamscape, where hearts belong.

Boundless joys float on the breeze,
In whispered moments, hearts find ease.
Together we roam, in radiant bliss,
Chasing the magic, sealed with a kiss.

Lightheartedness Amidst the Dark

Starlight twinkles in velvet skies,
Laughter rises, softly flies.
In shadows cast, joy finds a way,
Lightheartedness breaks through the gray.

Echoes of giggles, bright and clear,
Chasing away the lingering fear.
With every step, we light the night,
Turning darkness into delight.

Candles flicker, shadows dance,
In sweet moments, we take a chance.
Hand in hand, we twirl and spin,
Crafting magic from deep within.

In every heartbeat, joy ignites,
A spark of laughter, pure and bright.
Amidst the dark, we stand as one,
Finding light till the night is done.

Elysian Echoes Underneath the Blankets of Time

In the hush of hours, whispers blend,
Elysian echoes, a timeless friend.
Wrapped in comfort, moments sway,
Underneath the blankets, we drift away.

Each sigh a journey, soft and sweet,
In dreams held gently, our hearts meet.
Time unfolds like petals in bloom,
In the quiet embrace, we discover room.

Stars weave threads through fabric divine,
In the tapestry of hope, we intertwine.
With every memory, laughter aligns,
Beneath the blankets, the soul shines.

As shadows dance and daylight creeps,
These elysian echoes, forever keep.
Moments cherished, warm and kind,
In the heart's library, ever entwined.

Hidden Faces of Happiness in the Ether

Behind the clouds, joy softly glows,
Whispers of laughter, in secret flows.
A dance of shadows, in twilight's field,
Hidden faces, emotions revealed.

Amidst the silence, smiles take flight,
In every heartbeat, a flicker of light.
Gentle breezes, laughter's sweet song,
In the ether where dreamers belong.

Colors of sunset, softly they blend,
Fleeting moments, where sorrows end.
The sky holds secrets, a palette divine,
Hidden faces of joy, forever entwine.

In gardens of hope, where wishes bloom,
Threads of happiness weave through the gloom.
Each glimmering star, a tale to tell,
Hidden faces, where gladness dwells.

Through life's journey, we chase the light,
Finding joy in the softest sight.
In the embrace of the night's tender breath,
Hidden faces of happiness, defying death.

Chuckles Adrift Among Dreamy Embers

Flickering flames in the cozy night,
With whispers of joy, hearts take flight.
Chuckles adrift on a warm, soft breeze,
Among dreamy embers, the soul finds ease.

Laughter dances in the soft glow,
Carried along where the sweet dreams flow.
In the flick of a spark, a smile ignites,
Lost in the magic, the world feels right.

The essence of joy in each burning crest,
Chuckles unfurl, a playful jest.
Under the stars, with spirits set free,
Embers of laughter, our hearts in glee.

As shadows waltz with the moonlit hue,
We gather our tales, old and new.
Through giggles and sighs, we find our way,
Among dreamy embers, we long to stay.

In a soft cocoon of twinkling lights,
We share our dreams on those tender nights.
Chuckles adrift, a harmonious tune,
Binding us close under a watchful moon.

The Unobserved Rays of Delight in Night's Cloak

In the cloak of night, delight does gleam,
Unobserved rays, like whispers of dream.
Sparks of joy in the dark's embrace,
Illuminating paths in a tender space.

The stars keep secrets, they flicker and sway,
In their gentle glow, we find our way.
Under the velvet of midnight's kiss,
Unnoticed bursts of serene bliss.

A soft lullaby sings to our fears,
As laughter lingers, washing away tears.
In shadows painted with whispers of grace,
The unobserved rays find their rightful place.

Moments of wonder in twilight's hush,
Guided by starlight, a euphoric rush.
Invisible joy, like a delicate thread,
In the night's tapestry, softly spread.

With each pulse of the night, we feel alive,
In the unobserved rays, our spirits thrive.
Dancing in silence, where dreams take flight,
Delight finds a home, wrapped close in the night.

Yonder the Laughter in Shadows Entwined

In the realm of whispers, laughter lingers,
Yonder the echoes of joy through fingers.
Shadows entwined beneath the tree,
Where secrets are traded, wild and free.

Soft giggles weave through the evening air,
Hints of delight hiding everywhere.
In twilight's glow, where the stories unfold,
Yonder laughter sparkles, a sight to behold.

Beneath the stars in their shimmering flow,
We gather our dreams, let our spirits glow.
Every chuckle resonates, a sweet refrain,
In shadows entwined, joy dances and reigns.

The night is alive with tales to share,
Moments of bonding, beyond compare.
Yonder a glimpse of hope's gentle sheen,
In the laughter of shadows, all's serene.

As dawn's first light begins to creep,
Memories of laughter, a treasure to keep.
In shadows entwined, we continue to find,
The essence of joy that forever will bind.

Whispers of Laughter Beneath Twilight

In the hush of dusk, dreams take flight,
Soft giggles dance, igniting the night.
Stars wink above, a gentle guide,
As whispers of joy weave side by side.

Children's voices, a melody sweet,
Through shadows they run, on light feet.
Caught in the breeze, a secret shared,
With every laugh, a moment spared.

Gentle breezes carry their cheer,
Moonlit secrets held so dear.
In twilight's glow, we find our place,
Amidst playful sounds, a warm embrace.

Fireflies twinkle, like stars in the air,
Each blink a story, a joy laid bare.
Laughter entwines with the night so bright,
In whispers of laughter, pure delight.

Forever etched in the fabric of time,
These fleeting moments, a lonesome rhyme.
In the heart of twilight, unity sings,
With laughter's echo, our spirit takes wings.

Echoes of Joy in Starlit Corners

In corners where starlight gently gleams,
Laughter ricochets, carrying dreams.
Soft whispers of joy float on the breeze,
In the velvet night, hearts find their ease.

Footsteps dance in puddles of light,
As shadows play, creating delight.
With every giggle, the world feels bright,
In starlit corners, joy takes flight.

Secrets linger in the evening air,
As friendships blossom, fond and rare.
Echoes of memories stir in the night,
Painting the dark with colors of light.

A tapestry woven with laughter and grace,
In these moments, we find our place.
With stars as our witness, we spark the flame,
In echoes of joy, we'll never be the same.

So let the night wrap us in its embrace,
Each giggle a treasure, no time to replace.
In starlit corners where dreams intertwine,
We hold the essence of joy divine.

Radiant Grins Amidst Murmurs of Night

In the gentle glow of evening's calm,
Radiant grins weave a heartfelt balm.
Murmurs of night hum a soothing tune,
As joy spills freely beneath the moon.

Sparks of laughter light up the air,
Chasing away every worry and care.
In the stillness, smiles become a thread,
Binding us close, where all fears shed.

The warmth of friendship beneath the stars,
Scattered like jewels, they cure our scars.
In every chuckle, a promise anew,
Radiant grins shine through and through.

Murmurs of stories, soft and low,
Blend with the breeze, in a gentle flow.
In the hush of night, we find our way,
With laughter's embrace, we boldly sway.

In the magic of darkness, we're not alone,
With each joyful heartbeat, we've found our home.
Radiant grins amid night's sweet song,
Crafting the memories where we belong.

Glimmers of Happiness in Twilight's Embrace

As twilight descends, the world turns gold,
Glimmers of happiness quietly unfold.
In the softest light where shadows play,
Whispers of joy beckon, come what may.

Through laughter shared and tender glances,
Moments ignite in whimsical dances.
Each smile a sparkle, a radiant trace,
Glimmers of joy in twilight's embrace.

Those fleeting seconds, a treasure to keep,
In the silence of night, our hearts leap.
Under the canvas of stars so vast,
We savor the present, let worries pass.

In every rustle, in every sigh,
Glimmers of happiness float softly by.
With open hearts, we gather the night,
In the glow of twilight, everything feels right.

Hold onto these moments, so pure, so bright,
With laughter as our beacon, we take flight.
In twilight's embrace, where dreams intertwine,
Glimmers of happiness forever shine.

The Quiet Brightness of Hidden Laughter

In shadows where the secrets hide,
Soft giggles dance on whispers wide.
The night conceals the joyful sound,
In every corner, laughter found.

Heartbeats sync in playful cheer,
A world alive, yet no one near.
Where silence holds a vibrant tune,
And stars above sing soft, in June.

Beneath the glow of moonlit skies,
The echoes of our joy arise.
In stolen moments, we ignite,
The quiet brightness, pure delight.

With every glance and fleeting grin,
The hidden laughter calls us in.
A warmth that wraps, a gentle balm,
In shadows, life feels sweet and calm.

Together, in this sacred space,
We weave our dreams, our hearts embrace.
The quietness, a tender friend,
In laughter's light, we find, transcend.

Moonlit Grins Behind Closed Eyes

In twilight's hush, we hold our breath,
A world unseen, yet full of zest.
The silver glow speaks soft and low,
As moonlit grins begin to grow.

In dreams we paint with shades so bright,
Creating worlds that dance with light.
Behind closed eyes, we drift and sway,
In secret realms where bluebirds play.

With every sigh, our smiles unfold,
A tapestry of joys untold.
The night cradles our playful minds,
In soft embrace, the stars remind.

As shadows weave through quiet sighs,
The magic sparks, our spirits rise.
In tandem beats, our hearts align,
Embracing dreams in love's design.

So let the night carry us high,
To places where our laughter flies.
In moonlit grins, we find our way,
Through whispered tales till break of day.

Joyful Secrets in the Veil of Night

Amidst the dusk, our voices fade,
A treasure chest where dreams invade.
With every giggle softly shared,
The night hugs close what we've declared.

The stars conspire with silent glee,
Whispering tales to you and me.
In gentle waves, secrets unfold,
In joyful whispers, truth is bold.

Beneath the moon's protective gaze,
We dance through time, lost in a haze.
With every twinkle, hopes take flight,
In playful darkness, hearts unite.

Each moment lingers, vast and sweet,
A symphony of souls that meet.
In shadows deep, we leave no trace,
But memories of our secret place.

So let the night enfold our dreams,
With joyful secrets, bursting seams.
In every heartbeat, magic sings,
Embracing all that laughter brings.

Playful Whispers on the Edge of Slumber

As day gives way, the night ignites,
With playful whispers, soft delights.
On edges where our dreams take flight,
The hush of twilight, pure invite.

In gentle breezes, secrets flow,
Through starlit paths where wishes grow.
Each hush a promise, every sigh,
We sail through realms, just you and I.

With eyes alight, we chase the stars,
Navigating life, no fears or scars.
In this sweet ether, time stands still,
With whispered dreams, we find our will.

As shadows mingle with the dawn,
We dance in twilight until it's gone.
Our laughter lingers in the air,
A memory spun from dreams we share.

So let the night cradle our grace,
In playful whispers, we find our place.
Through slumber's edge, our hearts entwined,
In every secret wish defined.

Elusive Happiness in the Dim Light

In shadows soft, we seek the glow,
A fleeting spark, where dreams may flow.
The whispers fade, like echoes lost,
Yet hearts remain, despite the cost.

A smile flickers, just out of reach,
In corners dim, where silence can teach.
We chase the warmth, though cold winds bite,
Finding joy in the dimmest light.

Moments rare, like stars above,
Fleeting joy, a whisper of love.
We dance between sorrow and cheer,
Finding fleeting bliss, drawing near.

In every heart, a hidden flame,
A silent spark, yet none the same.
Through moments blurred, we hold on tight,
To elusive happiness, a secret light.

So let us dream in half-lit halls,
Where laughter fades, and shadow calls.
In search of joy, may we delight,
In elusive happiness, through the night.

Flickers of Fun Amongst Quiet Dreams

In the twilight, whispers play,
Gentle laughter, fading away.
A spark of joy, in silence found,
Echoing softly, a sweet sound.

In quiet corners, shadows dance,
Moments fleeting, a sweet chance.
We weave our dreams in twilight's hue,
Colors bright, yet seldom true.

Flickers of fun, like fireflies,
Twinkling low under starlit skies.
They guide our hearts on paths so bright,
Through quiet dreams, we find our light.

The world may hush, but joy will swell,
In memories where laughter dwells.
Each flicker a tale, a fleeting muse,
In quiet dreams, we cannot lose.

So let us cherish these moments rare,
Where laughter blooms in fragrant air.
Flickers of fun will always gleam,
Amongst the quiet of our dreams.

Pockets of Light in Dusky Universes

In dusky fields, the stars ignite,
Pockets of light, that pierce the night.
Each glimmer holds a story true,
Whispers of hope in skies so blue.

We wander through this cosmic dance,
Seeking meaning, a second chance.
In shadows deep, we gently tread,
Finding solace, where dreams are fed.

A universe vast, in darkness rife,
Yet hidden gems breathe signs of life.
Each tiny spark, a guiding sight,
In pockets of light, we find our might.

So let us gaze at the endless sky,
Drawn by the stars, we learn to fly.
For in these moments, we feel alive,
In dusky universes, we thrive.

Together we'll chase the cosmic streams,
Creating magic in our dreams.
Pockets of light will always lead,
To places unknown, where hearts are freed.

Hidden Ecstasy in the Depth of Night

In the depth of night, secrets lay,
Hidden ecstasy, in shadows play.
A world awake, yet so serene,
Whispers of joy, where few have been.

The moon hangs low, casting its glow,
In darkness deep, our desires flow.
Moments stolen beneath the stars,
Each breath ignites, though life leaves scars.

Hidden wonders, lost in the sighs,
Where silence speaks, and laughter lies.
In twilight's embrace, we seek delight,
Finding ecstasy in each soft bite.

A heartbeat shared, in stillness found,
Promises whispered, without a sound.
In secret places, love's sweet fight,
Reveals the ecstasy of the night.

So let us wander, hand in hand,
Through dusky paths, a magic land.
In hidden ecstasy, we unite,
Forever bound in the depth of night.

The Silent Symphony of Unvoiced Cheer

In whispers soft, the shadows dance,
With every glance, a fleeting chance.
The heartbeats hum a secret song,
Where silent joys have lingered long.

Amidst the quiet, laughter sways,
In tranquil grace, it finds its ways.
A symphony of thoughts unspun,
Reveals the warmth of life's sweet run.

With every smile that lights the night,
Unvoiced cheer takes silent flight.
In gentle moments, love will bloom,
As echoes fill the silent room.

Each glance a note, a tender thread,
Of moments shared, where hearts have led.
In hush of night, the spirit sings,
Of joy that's found in simple things.

Beneath the Veil of Night

Beneath the veil of twilight's grace,
The stars awake to claim their place.
In silver light, the world ignites,
As dreams ascend to dizzy heights.

The moon adorns the velvet sky,
A silent guardian drifting by.
In whispered secrets of the gloom,
The night enfolds in soft perfume.

While shadows twirl in gentle sway,
The heart finds peace at end of day.
Within the hush of solitude,
A tranquil spirit is renewed.

Here in the stillness, time unfolds,
With every heartbeat, stories told.
Beneath the veil where whispers lie,
Our hopes take flight, our worries die.

Lightness Blossoms

In fields where flowers gently sway,
The lightness blooms in bright array.
With laughter sweet, the breezes play,
And chase the heavy clouds away.

Petals dance on whispers light,
As sunbeams weave through morning bright.
Each moment glows, a vibrant hue,
A symphony of life anew.

From every heart, joy bursts alive,
In lightness, we learn how to thrive.
With every breath, delight unfolds,
As stories bloom in colors bold.

In open skies, the spirit soars,
To taste the freedom, love restores.
Lightness, like petals in the breeze,
Reminds us life can bring us ease.

Hidden Joys in the Quietude of Night

In the quietude where shadows play,
Hidden joys find their way to stay.
In silence thick, secrets unfold,
As dreams embrace the night so bold.

Each star a gem in infinite dark,
A spark that leaves a subtle mark.
In hushed reverie, hearts align,
To dance in rhythm, yours and mine.

With every sigh, the world retreats,
To cradle truths that time repeats.
In whispered hopes beneath the moon,
We find a melody, a tune.

The still of night calls forth the past,
With tender hands, we hold it fast.
In hidden joys, the spirit gleams,
And life collects our scattered dreams.

Glimmers of Hope in Enchanted Realms

In enchanted realms where shadows weave,
Glimmers of hope begin to breathe.
Through misty paths and starlit skies,
The heart learns how to rise and rise.

Each flicker dances with pure delight,
As dreams take flight in the soft night.
With every heartbeat, courage swells,
In whispered truths, our spirit dwells.

Through tangled woods and secret streams,
The light unveils our deepest dreams.
In every corner of the soul,
Glimmers of hope can make us whole.

In fabled lands where fairies tread,
And paths of crystal light are spread,
We find the courage to believe,
In glimmers that the heart can weave.

Laughter's Glint in the Abyss of Night

In shadows deep, where echoes play,
A spark of joy, a light of day.
Amid the dark, a giggle sings,
Wrapped in a cloak, of whispered wings.

Beneath the stars, a flicker bright,
Unraveling fears, restoring light.
The moonbeams dance, in playful cheer,
Laughter calls, the night draws near.

In corners dim, where silence fell,
A story spun, a jolly spell.
With every chuckle that takes flight,
Hope's glint shines through the endless night.

Voices weave, in giddy flight,
Painting dreams, banishing fright.
As shadows fade, and spirits soar,
Laughter's glint, forevermore.

Playful Whispers in the Forgotten Corners

In quiet nooks where secrets rise,
Soft voices play beneath the skies.
Hidden tales of joy and mirth,
Awaken dreams upon this earth.

Fleeting giggles, like gentle rain,
Brush the skin, delight the grain.
Every whisper holds a spark,
Mapping trails through the eternal dark.

Dance of shadows, twinkle bright,
Echoing laughter through the night.
Each corner long lost, now alive,
Playful whispers begin to thrive.

In memories spun, the heart takes flight,
Through forgotten lands, in pure delight.
Where silence lingers, joy will grow,
As playful whispers softly flow.

Enchanted Grins Beyond the Dusk

When twilight drapes the world anew,
Enchanted grins find me and you.
They bloom in silence, warm and bright,
Casting shadows in fading light.

In twilight's hold, magic ignites,
A spark of joy in starry nights.
Mischievous glances, playful glints,
Grinning wide, the heart repents.

As laughter rings, the night awakes,
Every grin a new path makes.
Beneath the moon's soft, watchful eye,
Joyful tales will ever fly.

In echoes of fun, our spirits soar,
To enchanted realms, forevermore.
With every grin, love's light is cast,
Beyond the dusk, a spell will last.

Joy's Lattice in the Stillness of Nightfall

In the stillness where dreams abide,
Joy weaves softly, a gentle guide.
Through quiet threads, laughter spins,
A lattice bright, where life begins.

Each night's embrace brings whispers sweet,
In harmony, our hearts will beat.
With every moment, joy takes flight,
Building bridges through the night.

Stars align, in blissful dance,
Inviting souls to take a chance.
Lost in time, our spirits blend,
Joy's lattice weaves, until the end.

When shadows speak, and silence reigns,
Through stillness, life's true magic gains.
Embrace the night, let worries cease,
In joy's warm lattice, find your peace.

Mirage of Merriment in Dim Light

In the dusk where shadows play,
Laughter dances, fades away,
Echoes linger, light confesses,
Whispers trapped in dark recesses.

Flickers of joy in twilight speak,
Memories bright, though voices weak,
A gentle sigh, a fleeting glance,
In the dimness, dreams still dance.

Underneath the moon's soft gaze,
Time slips by in hazy ways,
Colors blend, a sweet charade,
In twilight's grasp, the heart may wade.

Soft shadows wrap the evening tight,
Where mirth lingers, shining bright,
Moments stolen from the day,
In the dim light, we lose our way.

Yet in this haze, there lies a spark,
A glimpse of joy within the dark,
As laughter weaves its silk so fine,
In the mirage, our hearts align.

Hidden Gleams in the Quiet Hours

When the world rests, hushed and still,
Soft secrets emerge at will,
Glistening gems in muted light,
Whispered dreams take flight, take flight.

Faint glimmers on the edge of night,
Illuminate the endless plight,
In stillness found, the soul finds peace,
From weary thoughts, a sweet release.

In hidden nooks, laughter hides,
Amidst the calm, where magic bides,
Gentle echoes of what was,
Embrace us now without a cause.

Blushing stars in velvet skies,
Silent wishes, gentle sighs,
From ajar doors, warmth spills out,
Embracing all, erasing doubt.

So in these hours, soft and rare,
We find the light, we shed despair,
For hidden gleams, like fleeting stars,
Guide us home from distant scars.

Reflections of Delight in Hazy Mists

In morning's breath, a gentle glow,
Where echoes of delight still flow,
Misty veils conceal and reveal,
The tenderness that we can feel.

Reflections dance on dew-kissed grass,
Memories linger as moments pass,
Whispers of joy in the muted dawn,
Like fleeting dreams, they're never gone.

Clouded paths hold secrets dear,
Voices soft, yet crystal clear,
In hazy mists, our hearts unfold,
With stories shared and lives retold.

A tapestry woven in shifting light,
Each thread a memory, warm and bright,
In the silence, beauty flows,
In the mist, our wonder glows.

So let us wander through this haze,
Find delight in passing days,
For in each breath, reflections gleam,
A dance of joy within the dream.

Glimmers of Hope in the Twilight Realm

As day surrenders to night's embrace,
Hope flickers softly in that space,
Beneath the stars, we stake our claim,
In twilight's arms, we stay the same.

Golden hues fade to silver grace,
Dreams find a home in shadowed place,
With every heartbeat, whispers rise,
In the stillness, our spirits fly.

Through the twilight, colors weave,
Stories waiting for us to believe,
Each glimmer speaks of days to come,
In this realm, our hearts are one.

A gentle breeze carries our sighs,
While stars emerge in velvet skies,
With glimmers of hope, we take our stand,
Hand in hand, across the land.

So let the darkness wrap us tight,
For within it, we find our light,
In twilight's glow, our dreams unite,
Glimmers of hope in the softest night.

Soft Chuckles Beneath the Canopy of Night

Whispers drift on evening's breeze,
Stars above, like playful tease.
Laughter floats on moonlit streams,
Soft chuckles weave through gentle dreams.

Shadows dance on silken ground,
A symphony of night surrounds.
Crickets serenade the air,
In this realm, we shed our care.

Beneath the vast, celestial dome,
Hearts unite, we feel at home.
With every giggle, spirits rise,
Connected under velvet skies.

Echoes linger, soft and light,
Joyful whispers greet the night.
In the calm, our troubles cease,
Wrapped in laughter, purest peace.

So let the stars bear witness here,
To laughter, hope, and love so dear.
Together in this magic hour,
We'll cherish every fleeting flower.

Joy's Flicker in the Depths of Sleep

In the quiet, dreams unfold,
A flicker of warmth, a tale retold.
Joy dances lightly in our minds,
Innocent moments, purest finds.

Softly gleaming, visions play,
Woven tales in shades of gray.
Laughter echoes, gentle and sweet,
In this world where dreams compete.

Nightly wanderers take their flight,
From shadowed corners into light.
Joy's flicker ignites the soul,
In slumber's arms, we feel whole.

Beneath the folds of silken night,
Dreams take shape, a wondrous sight.
Every chuckle, every sigh,
In sleep's embrace, we learn to fly.

So let the night embrace our hearts,
Where joy ignites and never parts.
In the depths of sleep, we find,
A flicker of joy, intertwined.

Hidden Gleams of Laughter in Dreamscapes

In dreamscapes vast, where shadows blend,
Hidden gleams of laughter mend.
Whispers, twinkles, spark the night,
In this realm, pure delight.

Softly glows the moonlit mist,
Every giggle feels like bliss.
Footsteps light on phantom trails,
Echoes of our joyful tales.

With every wink, the darkness glows,
In secret places, laughter flows.
Floating dreams on buoyant air,
In hidden folds, we shed our care.

Dreamscapes hold a magic key,
Unlocking wild, sweet reverie.
Laughter bubbles, wild and free,
A symphony of jubilee.

So let us wander, blissfully lost,
Through the laughter, we are tossed.
In dreamscapes bright, we'll always gleam,
Where joy awakens every dream.

Reflections of Delight in Dusky Mists

In dusky mists, reflections gleam,
Delight dances, like a dream.
Whispers float on twilight's sigh,
Capturing moments that brush by.

Shades of laughter paint the night,
Mirroring joy, pure and bright.
With every glow, the shadows play,
In this haze, we drift away.

Sweet echoes chase the fading light,
In reflections, we take flight.
Every giggle, every tune,
Lifts our spirits, like a balloon.

The dusky veil unveils the heart,
Where laughter ends, love will start.
In the quiet, we find our grace,
In reflections, we embrace.

So let the mists make us anew,
In delight's arms, we'll see it through.
With every step, we'll softly sway,
Reflections guide us on our way.

Gleams of Delight Beneath the Surface

In shadows deep, where whispers play,
Bright dreams flicker, fade, then sway.
Beneath the calm, a hidden spark,
Gleams of joy ignite the dark.

With every wave, a secret thrill,
A gentle heart, a silent will.
Rippling softly, hope's embrace,
Chasing light in a silent space.

In quiet depths, the treasures lie,
Moments gleam, like stars in the sky.
Awakening with each soft breath,
In stillness blooms a dance with death.

Laughter echoes, joy's release,
Finding peace where sorrows cease.
Underneath, the currents weave,
Gleams of delight that we believe.

The surface still, a tranquil guise,
Yet underneath, the spirit flies.
In that realm, sweet wonders blend,
Gleams of delight that never end.

Subtle Radiance in the Dark's Embrace

When shadows fall and night unfolds,
A gentle warmth, the heart beholds.
Subtle radiance, softly glows,
Shining light where no one goes.

In every corner, secrets blend,
The quiet night, a faithful friend.
Stars twinkle softly, guiding hearts,
Illuminating all its parts.

Whispers dance on the evening breeze,
With every sigh, the soul finds ease.
In dark's embrace, serenity,
A subtle glow, so pure and free.

Echoes shimmer beneath the moon,
The world sleeps while the light is strewn.
In that calm, we find a trace,
Of subtle radiance's grace.

So let us linger, hold this night,
In shadows cradled, find our light.
For in the dark, we learn to see,
The subtle radiance that can be.

Silhouettes of Laughter at Dusk

As dusk descends, the shadows play,
Silhouettes dance at close of day.
With every laugh, the world ignites,
Painting joy in fading lights.

Children's giggles, a cheerful sound,
Echoing as the sun goes down.
Every smile, a spark of hope,
In twilight's glow, we learn to cope.

Beneath the trees, where dreams unite,
Laughter lingers, pure delight.
In silhouettes, we find our voice,
In every heartbeat, love rejoices.

With stars awakened, the night unfurls,
Soft whispers shared, as magic swirls.
In dusky hues, we glimpse the art,
Of silhouettes that touch the heart.

So let us savor all that's near,
In laughter's echo, we draw near.
At dusk's embrace, we come alive,
In silhouettes, our spirits thrive.

The Radiant Glow of Unseen Joy

In corners where the shadows lie,
A radiant glow that we can't deny.
Unseen joy dances in the air,
A gentle whisper, a silent prayer.

With every heartbeat, a spark ignites,
Illuminating dark, bringing light.
In hidden places, wonders bloom,
The quiet glow that chases gloom.

Soft moments weave through daily strife,
In simple acts, we find our life.
The glow that glimmers, pure and bright,
Filling hearts with warmth each night.

Though veiled by time, the truth remains,
In unseen joy, no soul restrains.
A vibrant pulse beneath the skin,
The radiant glow begins within.

So let us seek that inner fire,
In life's tapestry, we aspire.
For joy's embrace is always near,
The radiant glow that conquers fear.

Cheerful Hues in the Veiled Horizon

Golden rays peek through the mist,
A canvas bright where dreams exist.
Whispers of light paint the dawn,
New days wake, old fears are gone.

Fields of colors, wild and free,
Nature sings in harmony.
Joyful hearts dance in the breeze,
Life unfolds with effortless ease.

Buds of laughter gently bloom,
Chasing away the night's dark gloom.
Hope emerges, warm and pure,
In every shade, we find our cure.

Birds take flight, their spirits soar,
As sunlight opens every door.
With every hue, we come alive,
In cheerful shades, we thrive and strive.

So let the colors fill our days,
In playful patterns, bright displays.
Together we shall paint our way,
Through life's canvas, come what may.

Luminous Hearts Within the Velvet Shadows

In velvet nights, hearts softly glow,
Echoes of laughter ebb and flow.
Stars above, a watchful gaze,
Guiding dreams through night's dark maze.

Whispers linger in the air,
As secret joys we love to share.
Each heart glimmers with soft light,
Dispelling fears that haunt the night.

Friendship's warmth in shadowed light,
Fills the spaces, making bright.
Through every trial, love shall rise,
A glowing bond that never dies.

Together we weave tales untold,
In every heartbeat, love's pure gold.
With luminous threads, we paint the dark,
In velvet shadows, we leave our mark.

Beneath the veil, where dreams take flight,
Hearts will shimmer, fierce and bright.
In the quiet, our souls entwine,
Shining boldly, forever divine.

The Dance of Grins in the Obscure

In shadows deep, where secrets hide,
Grins emerge, a joyous guide.
Through the mist, we find our way,
Dancing freely, come what may.

Footsteps echo in the night,
With laughter shared, spirits ignite.
Every turn, a new surprise,
In the dark, our joy will rise.

Curious hearts, we roam the void,
Finding moments to be enjoyed.
In playful leaps, we chase the stars,
Our smiles brighten, healing scars.

A rhythm beats within our chests,
Together strong, we conquer quests.
With every grin, we break the gloom,
In the obscure, our spirits bloom.

So let us dance, both wild and free,
In the shadows, joyful glee.
With every step, we lose the fear,
In the darkness, our light is clear.

Bright Threads in the Fabric of Night

In the fabric of the night,
Threads of silver, woven bright.
Each star shines, a gentle spark,
Illuminating paths in the dark.

As whispers weave through silent skies,
Hope dances where the moonlight lies.
Dreams entwined with midnight's grace,
In every heart, a sacred space.

Through the stillness, stories hum,
A tapestry where we all come.
Bright threads connect us, hand in hand,
In the darkness, we shall stand.

Every moment stitched with care,
As we journey, love's thread we share.
In the quiet, bonds grow tight,
In the fabric of the night.

So let us weave with colors bold,
Every whisper, a tale retold.
Together we'll create our plight,
With bright threads, we'll craft the night.

Whispers of Laughter Beneath the Night

In shadows deep, where dreams take flight,
Soft whispers dance, a warm delight.
Stars twinkle bright, secrets unfold,
As laughter echoes, rich and bold.

Moonlight drapes the world in grace,
Each chuckle brightens the secret space.
With every glimpse, hearts ignite,
Beneath the night, pure joy takes flight.

In fleeting moments, joy is spun,
Threads of happiness, woven as one.
The night beholds a playful show,
As whispers of laughter gently flow.

Together we share this gentle breeze,
In every laugh, the spirit frees.
Beneath this sky, our hearts align,
In whispers of joy, our souls entwine.

So let us linger, let us play,
In night's embrace, we'll find our way.
With laughter soft, we'll dance and sway,
For in this moment, we'll forever stay.

Echoes of Joy in the Gloom

In corners dark, where shadows creep,
Soft echoes of joy, secrets to keep.
Laughter rises, a beacon bright,
Guiding us through the deepest night.

Amidst the gloom, we find our tune,
Harmonies rise like a glowing moon.
Each chuckle shared, a thread so fine,
Weaving hope in every line.

With every smile, we cast a spell,
In the dark, where sweet memories dwell.
Together we sing, our spirits lift,
In echoes of joy, we find our gift.

Holding hands, we brave the storm,
In shared laughter, we feel so warm.
Through shadows deep, we find the light,
Echoes of joy, our purest delight.

So let the gloom fade into night,
With every laugh, our hearts take flight.
In the silence, the joy will bloom,
As we dance in the essence of gloom.

Radiance Woven in Midnight Tapestries

Underneath the cloak of deep, dark skies,
Midnight weaves tales through whispered sighs.
Threads of silver, glimmers entwine,
Woven with care, in patterns divine.

Each star a stitch, a story told,
In rich hues of night, both brave and bold.
Through the fabric of dreams, we entwine,
Radiance shines, a light so fine.

In quiet corners, the shadows play,
As midnight dances, night turns to day.
With every heartbeat, the stories flow,
In the tapestry's embrace, we'll grow.

Layered whispers, secrets unfold,
A warmth in the night, more precious than gold.
In these moments, magic sings,
Radiance woven on midnight wings.

So let us gather, hand in hand,
In midnight's glow, forever we stand.
Crafting laughter, a vibrant sea,
In the tapestry of you and me.

Flickers of Grin in Starlit Veils

Under the stars, where shadows play,
Flickers of grins light up the way.
With every twinkle, joy ignites,
In starlit veils, the heart delights.

Whispers travel through the cool night air,
Laughter dances without a care.
In tiny glances, secrets shared,
Flickers of grin, as hearts bared.

Moonbeams fall, painting our dreams,
In laughter's glow, nothing's as it seems.
Together we weave, side by side,
In this starlit journey, our hearts collide.

With every chuckle, the night grows bright,
In playful echoes, we find our light.
In the magic of now, we'll forever stay,
In flickers of grin, we find our way.

So let us linger, the night awaits,
In starlit veils, love suffocates.
With every grin, we paint the skies,
Under the stars, where pure joy lies.

Grinning Shadows on the Horizon of Dreams

Beyond the dusk, where shadows play,
A whisper stirs, night greets the day.
With every laugh, the darkness sighs,
In the dreams that dance with open eyes.

Flickering hopes in twilight's embrace,
Chasing the past, a fleeting trace.
The horizon glimmers, secrets untold,
As grinning shadows wrap us in gold.

Each heartbeat echoes through the night,
Illuminated by world's soft light.
In the silence, we find our way,
Through grinning shadows, night fades to day.

In every corner where fears reside,
Hope will blossom, bare and wide.
With laughter ringing, our spirits soar,
Grinning shadows beckon evermore.

So let us roam where dreams ignite,
Chasing horizons, hearts taking flight.
As shadows glide, we join the dance,
Embracing the magic of chance.

Laughter's Echo in the Quiet Abyss

In the silence where sorrows dwell,
Laughter rises, casting a spell.
Echoes linger in the still night,
Illuminating shadows, ghostly light.

The abyss whispers secrets within,
A vibrant world beneath the skin.
With every giggle, the darkness sways,
In laughter's echo, hope conveys.

Moments fleeting, like stars that fade,
Joy interlaces where dreams invade.
In the nothingness, a spark ignites,
Laughter unfurls to pierce the nights.

So when shadows cloak the heart's domain,
Laugh aloud, let go the pain.
In every chuckle, the abyss will glow,
A beacon of warmth when time feels slow.

For laughter's echo can heal the deep,
Awakening dreams from their silent sleep.
In the quiet abyss, let voices fly,
For joy will rise, and shadows die.

Starlight's Kiss on Invisible Smiles

In the twilight where dreams collide,
Starlight dances, a cosmic guide.
Soft kisses grace the hidden face,
Invisible smiles in an endless space.

Glistening whispers on the breeze,
Carrying joy, hearts find their ease.
Moments captured, like fireflies bright,
Starlight's embrace ignites the night.

Through the darkness, a gentle sigh,
Promising warmth from the night sky.
Invisible smiles light up the dark,
Each starlit kiss leaves a glowing mark.

In silence, we feel the magic swell,
A tapestry woven, a secret spell.
With every breath, the universe beams,
Starlight's kiss dances in our dreams.

So look to the heavens, let your heart roam,
For in starry whispers, you'll find your home.
Invisible smiles, forever they'll stay,
Guiding us softly, lighting the way.

The Subtle Art of Hidden Happiness

In the corners where shadows rest,
Happiness hides, a quiet guest.
With subtle grace, it softly sighs,
In the fleeting moments, bliss implies.

Behind the laughter, a secret dance,
In each curve of life, we take a chance.
Fleeting whispers from the soul's depth,
Bringing smiles with every breath.

Through tangled paths and winding ways,
Hidden joy in ordinary days.
A gentle thought, a warmth so near,
The art of happiness dwells here.

In silent corners, where dreams converge,
Let hope take root, and happiness surge.
With every breath, let joy unfold,
In unseen places, the heart grows bold.

For happiness waits, not loud, nor brash,
In soft encounters, it's found in a flash.
Embrace the subtle, let your heart sing,
In hidden happiness, life's true offering.

Playful Visions in the Twilight Realm

In twilight's glow where shadows dance,
Whispers of dreams take their chance.
Colors merge in a soft embrace,
Magic unfolds in this secret place.

Stars awaken, twinkling so bright,
Guiding the wanderers through the night.
Laughter echoes like a gentle breeze,
Every heart pairs with joy that frees.

Dancing with fireflies under the moon,
Nature's song hums a lovely tune.
Fleeting moments in the soft air,
Here we find wonder beyond compare.

A canvas painted with hues of gold,
Stories of magic yet untold.
Each shadow plays in the evening's light,
Inviting dreams to take their flight.

In this realm where time stands still,
Hope and wonder begin to fill.
Playful visions in the twilight glow,
Unraveling secrets of long ago.

Tidbits of Joy Amid the Unseen

Beneath the surface, joy resides,
In quiet corners where hope abides.
Gentle laughter floats through the air,
Hidden treasures waiting to share.

Moments of kindness bloom like flowers,
Unseen wonders unfold in the hours.
A child's giggle, a soft embrace,
Lifting spirits in this sacred space.

Sunlight dapples through the trees,
Nature's choir sings sweet jubilee.
Tiny wonders in the everyday,
Joyful tidbits join the fray.

Shadows dance as dusk drifts near,
Fleeting joys embraced with cheer.
In the silence, whispers are heard,
The magic of laughter, love's soft word.

Amid the unseen, hearts align,
In shared moments, love intertwines.
Each delicious breath, a gift to hold,
A tapestry of joy that unfolds.

The Melodies of Laughter in Silent Spaces

In silent spaces, laughter resides,
Echoing softly like gentle tides.
Melodies weave through the quiet air,
Uniting hearts with a tender flair.

Each giggle dances on the breeze,
Bringing warmth in moments that please.
Silent chuckles, a secret shared,
Binding souls who truly cared.

Beneath the stars, a hush will fall,
Yet laughter rises, breaking the wall.
In these still moments, we find our way,
The sweetest joy of night and day.

In cozy gatherings and whispered notes,
Life finds rhythm, the heart emotes.
Every smile a secret embrace,
The melodies linger in this space.

With each glance, a story unfolds,
In laughter's glow, we break the molds.
Silent spaces sing of the past,
In laughter's arms, we are held fast.

Radiance Caressed by Nightfall's Touch

As night descends, the world glows bright,
Radiance dances in the soft twilight.
Stars awaken, whispering true,
Caressed by dreams, the skies turn blue.

Moonlight spills like silver lace,
Enchanting the earth with a gentle grace.
Each twinkle tells tales of old,
Wonders of night, a sight to behold.

Soft shadows play on the velvet ground,
In every silence, beauty is found.
Nature's heartbeat slows to a hum,
Wrapped in the night, we're never numb.

With every breath, the universe sighs,
Cradled in starlight, we rise and rise.
The night embraces, a tender hold,
Instilling warmth as the air turns cold.

In radiance caressed by nightfall's kiss,
Dreams and hopes merge in perfect bliss.
Under the cosmos, we find our spark,
Guided forever through the dark.

Unseen Smirks Among the Stars

In the stillness of night, they shine,
Whispers of light in a vast divine.
Hidden grins in the cosmic dance,
Each twinkle tells tales of chance.

Beyond the reach of earthly despair,
Stars share secrets in silent air.
Together they weave a tapestry bright,
Flickers of joy in the endless night.

Across the void, they freely glance,
Mirthful glimmers in a timeless trance.
While we gaze, so small and meek,
Unseen smirks, the universe speaks.

A galaxy's breath, serene and slow,
Infinite wonders that ebb and flow.
In every spark, a moment's bliss,
A universe waiting for us to kiss.

So next time you find yourself lost,
Look up to the sky, no matter the cost.
For in those stars, the laughter lies,
Unseen smirks in the vastest skies.

Elysian Laughter Echoing in Esoteric Ways

In realms where the light of laughter dwells,
Joyful echoes in enchanted spells.
A symphony of voices, pure and bright,
Resounding softly in the moon's light.

The whispers float on the evening breeze,
Entwined mysteries beneath the trees.
Soft giggles break through the heavy mist,
An ethereal touch by the twilight kissed.

Melodies dance in the cool night air,
In every heartbeat, something rare.
Elysian dreams take shape and sway,
As laughter echoes in esoteric ways.

A hidden world where spirits play,
In the gentle folds of the golden day.
Whimsical sounds, a lullaby's grace,
Inviting all to join in the chase.

Tender moments linger, pure and free,
Elysian laughter, a sweet decree.
In echoes, we find our souls align,
In joy's embrace, forever entwined.

The Gentle Gleam of Elation in Darkness

In shadows deep, where silence breathes,
A gentle gleam of hope weaves.
Hints of joy in the muted light,
Shimmering softly, holding tight.

Colors dance in the pitch of night,
Flickers of elation, pure delight.
In the vast unknown, we dare to seek,
The gentle gleam that speaks so meek.

Through the veil of sorrow, it shines through,
Illuminating dreams, fresh and new.
A guiding star in the darkest hour,
Awakening the heart with silent power.

As we wander through trails unknown,
Familiar faces are often shown.
The gentle gleam, our compass bright,
Leading us home through the quiet night.

In every heartbeat, in every sigh,
It lifts us up as we learn to fly.
The elation found in this midnight glow,
Is the warmth of love we come to know.

Laughter's Shadow on a Canvas of Dreams

Upon the canvas where dreams unfold,
Laughter's shadow in colors bold.
Each stroke a memory, warm and bright,
A playful spirit igniting the night.

With every chuckle and every cheer,
Life's tender moments so crystal clear.
Shadows swirl like leaves in the breeze,
Creating worlds where the heart finds ease.

A palette of joy, a splash of glee,
In the artistry of you and me.
Echoes of laughter wage a sweet fight,
Imprinting dreams on the canvas of light.

In every shadow that softly slides,
Lives a story where happiness hides.
Crafted like music in vibrant hues,
A tapestry woven from love's muse.

So gather ye moments, both small and grand,
Paint your own journey, take a stand.
For laughter's shadow forever beams,
On the canvas of vibrant dreams.

The Glow of Inner Joy in Darkened Corners

In shadows deep, a flicker shines,
A spark of mirth where silence dines.
Lost in the night, the heart will glow,
A treasure bright, even when low.

Whispers dance like fireflies,
In hidden nooks, where laughter lies.
Soft echoes bounce off weary walls,
Reminding us, joy always calls.

As daylight fades, the stars awake,
In quiet bliss, the soul will shake.
Awakening dreams in hushed repose,
To find the light where no one goes.

A candle's flicker, a gentle tease,
Bringing comfort on the breeze.
In corners damped by time and care,
Inner joy blooms, fragile and rare.

So let us seek what's lost in shade,
In gentle hearts, where hope is laid.
For in the dark, we learn to see,
The glow of joy that sets us free.

Epic Tales of Laughter Between Dreams

Beneath the stars, the laughter flows,
In whispered tales, the spirit glows.
Where dreams entwine with joy's refrain,
Epic stories born of playful gain.

In twilight's grasp, the heart takes flight,
As giggles dance through velvet night.
The world transforms in shades of glee,
A canvas bright for you and me.

Adventures sparked in vivid hues,
A tapestry of wondrous views.
With every laugh, the dream unfolds,
A saga rich, as daylight holds.

Echoes linger in the silent air,
Each tale a bridge that we can share.
In hidden realms where laughter gleams,
A world awaits within our dreams.

So join the dance, let spirits soar,
In epic tales, we'll seek for more.
For laughter's light, our hearts embrace,
In dreams we find our sacred space.

Faint Grins Beneath a Gloomy Mosaic

In shadowed hues, the whispers play,
Faint grins flicker through the gray.
Beneath the weight of heavy skies,
A quiet joy in mischief lies.

Each broken piece tells tales of woe,
Yet hidden smiles begin to grow.
In every crack, a story shines,
As light breaks through, our heart aligns.

Mosaic shards, a patchwork life,
Amidst the pain, the joy is rife.
In deeper depths, where shadows creep,
We find our light within the deep.

Beneath the gloom, a spark ignites,
Turning sorrow into delights.
For even in the darkest night,
Faint grins reveal the coming light.

So let us dance amidst despair,
Embrace the joy that lingers there.
In every fragment, hope can gleam,
Beneath the mosaic, we find our dream.

Serendipity's Light in Midnight Reflections

In quiet hours, the world will pause,
Reflections gleam with nature's laws.
Serendipity sings its tune,
Underneath a soft, watchful moon.

In midnight's cloak, the heart takes flight,
Chasing shadows, seeking light.
Unexpected paths begin to show,
Leading us where wildflowers grow.

Soft whispers cradle dreams anew,
In moments shared, as stars break through.
Fate's gentle hand guides our way,
In joy's embrace, we shall not sway.

The stillness deep, the journey wide,
In every turn, let hope abide.
For serendipity finds its place,
In heartbeats quick, in warm embrace.

So cherish nights where dreams collide,
In midnight's arms, let love abide.
For in those moments, pure and bright,
We find our way, our inner light.

The Bright Side of Twilight's Embrace

In the fading light, dreams take flight,
Shadows dance with the fading sun.
Stars begin to twinkle bright,
Whispers of night have just begun.

Colors blend in a gentle kiss,
The horizon glows, a soft delight.
Embers of dusk bring a fleeting bliss,
As day gracefully meets the night.

Soft breezes carry secrets untold,
Crickets sing in a melodic tune.
Embraced by twilight, brave and bold,
We find our hearts beneath the moon.

A tapestry woven of hope and dreams,
Painting the sky in hues sublime.
In twilight's hold, nothing is as it seems,
Each moment a treasure, a glimpse of time.

Hushed Joys in the Edges of Reality

In corners of thought where shadows play,
Hushed joys linger like softest sighs.
Glimmers of truth in the light of day,
Hold the universe in quiet eyes.

Reality flickers, a fragile dance,
With every heartbeat, life whispers low.
Finding magic in each fleeting chance,
Where the river of dreams starts to flow.

Beneath the surface, the secrets lie,
A symphony born in silence found.
With every tear, with every cry,
They weave a fabric, resilient and sound.

In the edges of light, we dare to roam,
Chasing the echoes of what could be.
With every step, we inch toward home,
Finding joy in shared reverie.

Mirth Unraveled in Midnight's Hold

In midnight's clasp, laughter lies,
Veils of dreams drift soft and sweet.
Echoes shimmer in starry skies,
Unraveled joy at our dancing feet.

Moonlight sprinkles the earth with glee,
Playing tricks on sleepy eyes.
Whispers of magic, wild and free,
Unfurl in the silence, a sweet surprise.

Every heartbeat is a gentle chime,
Curtains of night draw close and tight.
In this moment, we feel sublime,
With mirth unraveled in the night.

The world may sleep, but we ignite,
Fires of wonder in the darkened air.
Bound by laughter, we take flight,
In midnight's hold, we find our flair.

Whimsy Wrapped in Soft Hues of Night

In soft hues of night, whimsy thrives,
Glimmers of gold in twilight's embrace.
Where laughter and joy effortlessly dives,
And the world twirls in a playful space.

Gentle breezes weave tales of delight,
Secrets of starlight begin to unfold.
Whimsy dances in shadows bright,
Embracing the hearts that dare to be bold.

In this canvas of dreams, we paint our song,
With brushes dipped in twilight's glow.
Every moment, where we belong,
Whispers of night, guiding us slow.

In this realm where magic flows,
We intertwine with the essence of night.
Wrapped in enchantment, our spirits know,
That whimsy's warmth is our guiding light.

The Unseen Dance of Glee in the Gloom

In shadows deep, joy spins a thread,
Whispers of laughter where sorrow has fled.
Twinkling eyes in the darkened embrace,
Finding bright sparks in a muted space.

A flicker of light in forgotten dreams,
Turning the night into radiant streams.
Gleeful hearts in the depths do sway,
In the unseen dance, they melt fears away.

The moon casts a glow on the smiling beams,
Filling the air with the sweetest themes.
Footsteps of hope on dampened ground,
In gloom's gentle hold, true joy is found.

Through the mist, a melody sings,
Carried on whispers, on soft, silken wings.
Each note a promise, a secret untold,
In the unseen dance, life's beauty unfolds.

So let the shadows hold their sweet play,
For joy can be found in the night's soft sway.
In the unseen dance, we twirl and glide,
In each fleeting moment, let laughter reside.

Fleeting Moments of Bliss Beneath the Stars

Beneath the vast dome where starlight glows,
Moments of bliss like a river flows.
Soft whispers carried on a gentle breeze,
Making time pause, putting hearts at ease.

In the stillness, the world takes a breath,
Cherishing life, defying the death.
Glimmers of joy in the night's embrace,
Fleeting yet timeless, each luminous trace.

A sparkle in eyes, a laugh in the air,
Memories crafted with love and with care.
Every heartbeat echoes in rhythm divine,
As fleeting moments with starlight align.

Together we stand, with wonder ablaze,
In the soft glow of the celestial haze.
A tapestry woven, a shimmering art,
In fleeting moments, we find the heart.

So let's seize the night as it softly unfolds,
In the company of stars, our stories retold.
Every glance shared, a beautiful thread,
In fleeting moments, true bliss is spread.

The Secret Garden of Cheerful Echoes

In a hidden nook where laughter nests,
Cheerful echoes dance, bringing gentle rests.
Petals of joy in the sunlight's kiss,
Greet all who wander seeking their bliss.

The breeze carries secrets of stories past,
In this garden of cheer, where moments last.
Blooming with warmth, each flower tongue-tied,
In childhood whispers, sweet dreams abide.

Colors explode in a vibrant parade,
Painting the pathways where shadows fade.
Laughter like music fills the fragrant air,
In this secret haven, free from despair.

Together we gather, hands intertwined,
Finding the treasures that life has designed.
Echoes of kindness, the warmth of a smile,
In the garden of cheer, let's rest for a while.

So roam through the blooms, as hope intertwines,
In each cheerful echo, true happiness shines.
A secret garden where spirits can play,
In the laughter of others, we find our way.

Efforts of Bubbles in Moonlit Waters

In moonlit waters, bubbles take flight,
Glimmering softly in the star-studded night.
Each rise is a wish, a fleeting delight,
Carried away on the waves of sheer light.

Dancing and twirling, a fragile ballet,
Efforts of laughter in silvery spray.
Melodies echo as ripples unfold,
In the heart of the night, secrets retold.

Floating on dreams where the cool waters sigh,
Bubbles of joy float up toward the sky.
Each one a treasure, a moment so bright,
In the softness of dusk, painted in white.

As they burst open, they sing of delight,
Whispers of freedom in pure moonlit sight.
In those simple efforts, true magic can be,
In bubbles of laughter, we find harmony.

So let us cherish these moments we share,
For life is like bubbles, delicate and rare.
In moonlit waters, where hearts intertwine,
Each effort of glee becomes simply divine.

Lighthearted Spirits on the Edge of Thought

In the morning glow, we rise anew,
With laughter's echo and skies so blue.
Thoughts like bubbles, floating free,
A dance of joy, just you and me.

Chasing dreams on a gentle breeze,
Whispers of secrets among the trees.
We giggle softly, no need to rush,
In moments shared, we feel the hush.

The sunbeams tickle our curious minds,
In every shadow, a treasure finds.
Bright like stars, we laugh and play,
Embracing the magic of the day.

With every step, a skip, a spin,
Celebrating small wins that draw us in.
The world's a canvas, we paint it bright,
Our spirits dance like beams of light.

So let us frolic on paths untrod,
Hand in hand, feeling the odd.
With lighthearted glee, we tread with grace,
In the extraordinary, we find our place.

Jolly Whispers in the Dreaming Shadows

In twilight's kiss, we softly glide,
With jolly whispers, our hearts are wide.
Dreams entwined in the evening air,
Laughter echoes, a sweet affair.

Among the shadows, secrets bloom,
Frolicsome wishes dispel the gloom.
Stars are winking, a playful tease,
Our voices mingling with rustling leaves.

With every chuckle, the night grows bright,
Adventures waiting in moon's soft light.
We paint the dark with colors bold,
In dreaming shadows, stories unfold.

The world is quiet, alive with grace,
In whispered tales, we find our place.
Let's gather memories like precious stones,
In jolly whispers, we hear our own tones.

So come, dear friend, let's laugh and sing,
With dreams and joy, we'll take to wing.
In the realm of wonder, let's softly tread,
With jolly whispers, our hearts are fed.

The Gleeful Heart in Desolate Quietude

In solitude's arms, a heart finds cheer,
Gleeful whispers, no need to fear.
In silence deep, we bloom like flowers,
Embracing moments, lingering hours.

The echoes of laughter fill empty space,
In quietude, joy finds its place.
With every breath, a sweet refrain,
Creating music from gentle pain.

Beneath the stillness, a vibrant beat,
Life dances softly, a rhythmic feat.
With gleeful spirit, we chase the day,
In desolate corners, we laugh and play.

Palettes of wonder in muted hues,
We paint our thoughts with delightful views.
Each heartbeat a treasure, we cherish true,
In the gleeful heart, the world feels new.

So let us gather, embrace the calm,
In quietude, we find our balm.
With joy as our guide, we rise and soar,
In a humble heart, we are never poor.

Slumbering Silences of Laughter Await

In twilight's embrace, a hush descends,
Slumbering silences, where laughter lends.
In the stillness, a tale unfolds,
Of dreams that shimmer like threads of gold.

The night wraps gently, a soft cocoon,
Whispers of joy beneath the moon.
In every shadow, giggles bloom,
A secret garden to chase away gloom.

With stars as scribes, we write our fate,
In laughter's arms, we celebrate.
Each chuckle lingers, a sweet refrain,
In slumbering silences, we break the chain.

The world may pause, but hearts beat loud,
In silent moments, we stand proud.
With laughter waiting, we share delight,
In the embrace of the starry night.

So hold my hand, let's dream and play,
In laughter's light, we'll find our way.
With slumbering silences, we rise and wake,
In joy and wonder, together we take.

www.ingramcontent.com/pod-product-compliance
Ingram Content Group UK Ltd.
Pitfield, Milton Keynes, MK11 3LW, UK
UKHW030916221224
452712UK00008B/1177